From rooms to houses: multi-family and single-family houses among the Minangkabau in Sumatra, Indonesia

Marcel Vellinga

9. Staffel/Jagdgeschwader 26

9. Staffel/Jagdgeschwader 26

The Battle of Britain Photo Album of Luftwaffe Bf 109 Pilot Willy Fronhöfer

Compiled by John Vasco

Schiffer Military History
Atglen, PA

Dustjacket artwork by Steve Ferguson, Colorado Springs, CO.

Book design by Robert Biondi.

Library of Congress Catalog Number: 2005920765.

Printed in China.
ISBN: 0-7643-2335-0

We are always looking for people to write books on new and related subjects. If you have an idea for a book, please contact us at the address below.

Published by Schiffer Publishing Ltd.
4880 Lower Valley Road
Atglen, PA 19310
Phone: (610) 593-1777
FAX: (610) 593-2002
E-mail: Info@schifferbooks.com.
Visit our web site at: www.schifferbooks.com
Please write for a free catalog.
This book may be purchased from the publisher.
Please include $3.95 postage.
Try your bookstore first.

In Europe, Schiffer books are distributed by:
Bushwood Books
6 Marksbury Ave.
Kew Gardens
Surrey TW9 4JF
England
Phone: 44 (0)20 8392-8585
FAX: 44 (0)20 8392-9876
E-mail: Bushwd@aol.com.
Free postage in the UK. Europe: air mail at cost.
Try your bookstore first.

Introduction

This work, of completely original photographs from Willy Fronhöfer, was made possible by the generous co-operation of Dave Brocklehurst and Mike Llewellyn, MBE, of the Kent Battle of Britain Museum in Hawkinge. The photographs were deposited with them some time ago and put fully at their disposal for the benefit of the museum. Upon seeing them, I felt that the only way to do the photographs full justice was in book form, with the additional caveat of the author proceeds from the book going to assist the ongoing upkeep of the museum. I am therefore grateful that this opportunity has arisen for this private collection of photographs to be made available to those with a keen interest in the aviation history of the Battle of Britain.

What is unusual about this work is that it is not simply a long procession of various views of several aircraft (although there are undoubtedly many who would wish to see that!). Instead, it is a short photo-history of one Luftwaffe fighter *Staffel*, predominantly showing the Battle of Britain period, up to the point when Willy Fronhöfer belly-landed his Bf 109 E-4, Yellow 10, W. Nr. 1184, at Jubilee Hall Farm, Ulcombe, on 31st August 1940 following combat with Pilot Officer Colin Gray of 54 Squadron. The photographs record, therefore, not only aircraft, but personalities of the *Staffel*, both flying and ground personnel; scenes of daily life; the devastation found as the *Staffel* advanced through occupied territory; the enemy aircraft found destroyed or abandoned, and a population made transient by the horror of war. It is a unique, albeit brief, insight into a very small section of the German war machine as it enjoyed unparalleled success in its push across western Europe in the spring and summer of 1940. I am grateful to Dave Brocklehurst and Mike Llewellyn, MBE, for making this possible.

9. *Staffel, Jagdgeschwader* 26

9. *Staffel*'s formation in September 1939 included a complement of personnel drafted in from II. *Gruppe Zerstörergeschwader* 26. The first *Staffelkapitän* was Gerhard Schöpel. The *Staffel* moved to Essen-Mülheim in November 1939, and were stationed there when the western campaign commenced on 10th May 1940. From then on the *Staffel* led what could be called almost a nomadic existence with frequent changes of base. 13th May saw a move to Mönchen-Gladbach, then to Peer on the 17th, Beauvechain on 19th, and Chièvres on the 27th. June saw a move to La Capelle on the 4th, Les Thilliers on the 13th, Villacoublay on the 17th, and back to Mönchen-Gladbach on the 22nd. From there they moved to Döberitz on 1st July, and finally Caffiers on 21st July, their base for operations against England during the summer of 1940 before moving to Abbeville-Drucat in November.

During his service with 9th *Staffel* in 1940, Willy Fronhöfer lodged claims three aerial victories. On 15th May he claimed a Mureaux 115 over Löwen; during the Dunkirk evacuation he claimed a Spitfire west of Dunkirk, and on 15th August in the early evening he claimed a Hurricane in the Folkestone area. His tussle with Colin Gray on 31st August however resulted not in a further victory claim, but a long period of captivity. Willy Fronhöfer was one of the fortunate members of his *Staffel* to survive the war; many of his comrades would not in the Battle of Britain and the campaigns to come.

The Photographs

Aircraft

This section shows several aircraft of 9. *Staffel*. Of particular interest, noted in recent publications concerning the *Staffel*, are the two different styles of the 9. *Staffel* emblem. The earlier 'Hellhound' emblem, in simple form with no embellishments, can be seen. Also, darker streaks can be seen on another variation of the early emblem. The later version shows a much fuller-bodied Hellhound, sometimes outlined, sometimes with demarcation lines between the wing and the body. Speculation abounds with regard to the colours employed. Recent commentary leans towards the emblem being in both red and black, at different times, and there is sufficient evidence in the photographs to support both contentions. On the later version, the mouth, tongue and ears have more intricate detail, and the odd photograph shows the use of more colours in the added detail. The *Geschwader* emblem of the stylised 'S' appears on the port side of all of the aircraft with the early style camouflage of light blue up the majority of the fuselage side. However, one photograph, of 'Yellow 3', with mottle down the port fuselage side shows no *Geschwader* emblem carried. The starboard side views also do not show 100% conformity. Whereas most views show the *Geschwader* emblem on the starboard side when the photographs permits, 'Yellow 8' that ended up in a hedge quite clearly does not carry the *Geschwader* emblem on the starboard side. Another interesting marking is the instructions for groundcrew ahead of the exhausts on the port side on some aircraft: 'Fullung 50% Wasser 50% Glykol 1,5 Schutzöl'. It was not a common occurrence for this kind of instruction to be seen on operational Bf 109s. As would be expected, the photographs show the fitment of both machine guns and 20mm. cannon in the wings, and also the two styles of cockpit canopy seen in 1940.

VDM

Füllung
50 l Wasser
50 l Glykol
1,5 Schutzöl

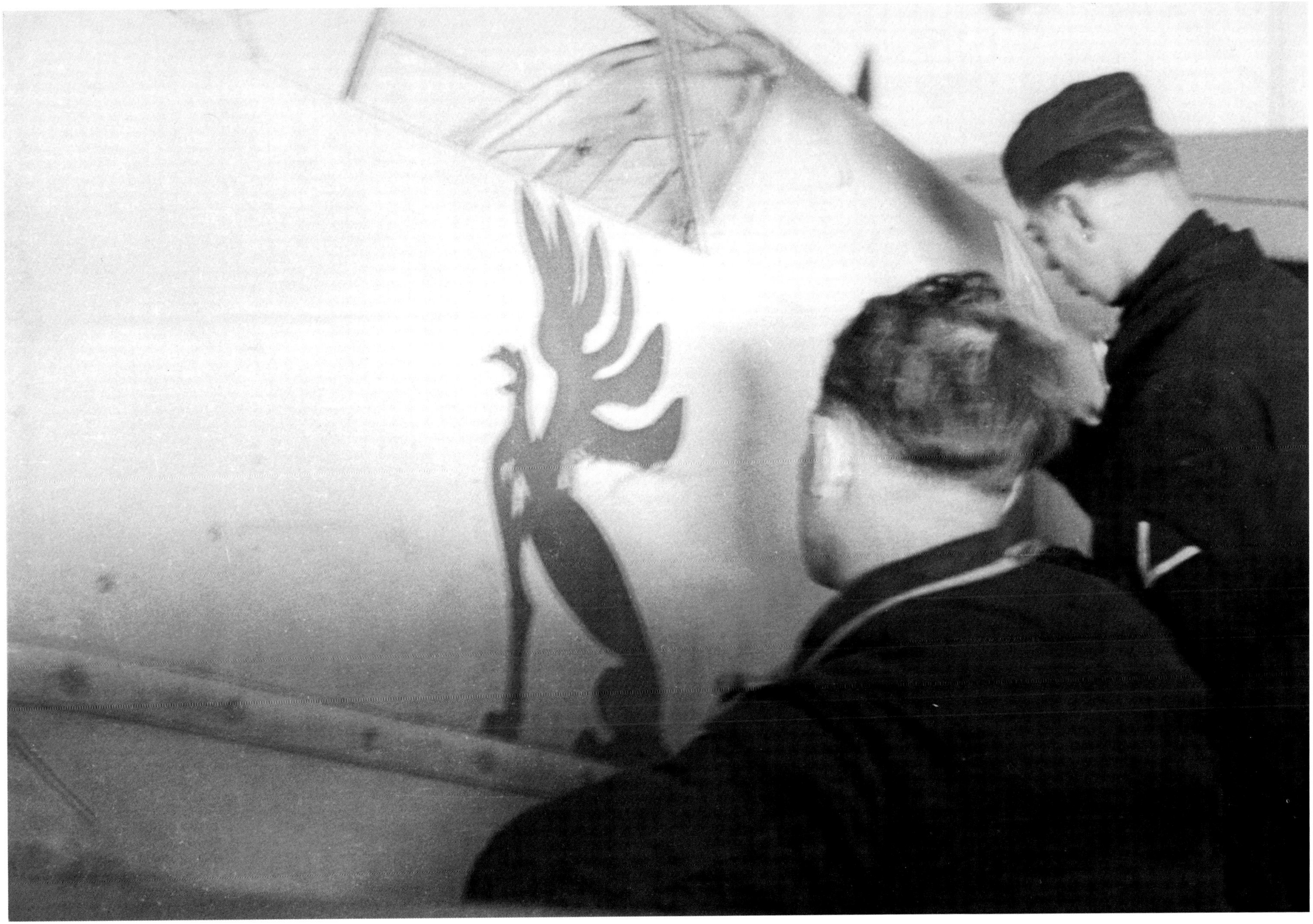

3

Buildings

This short section shows some of the damage inflicted on cities during the western campaign. The photographs speak for themselves and need no further comment.

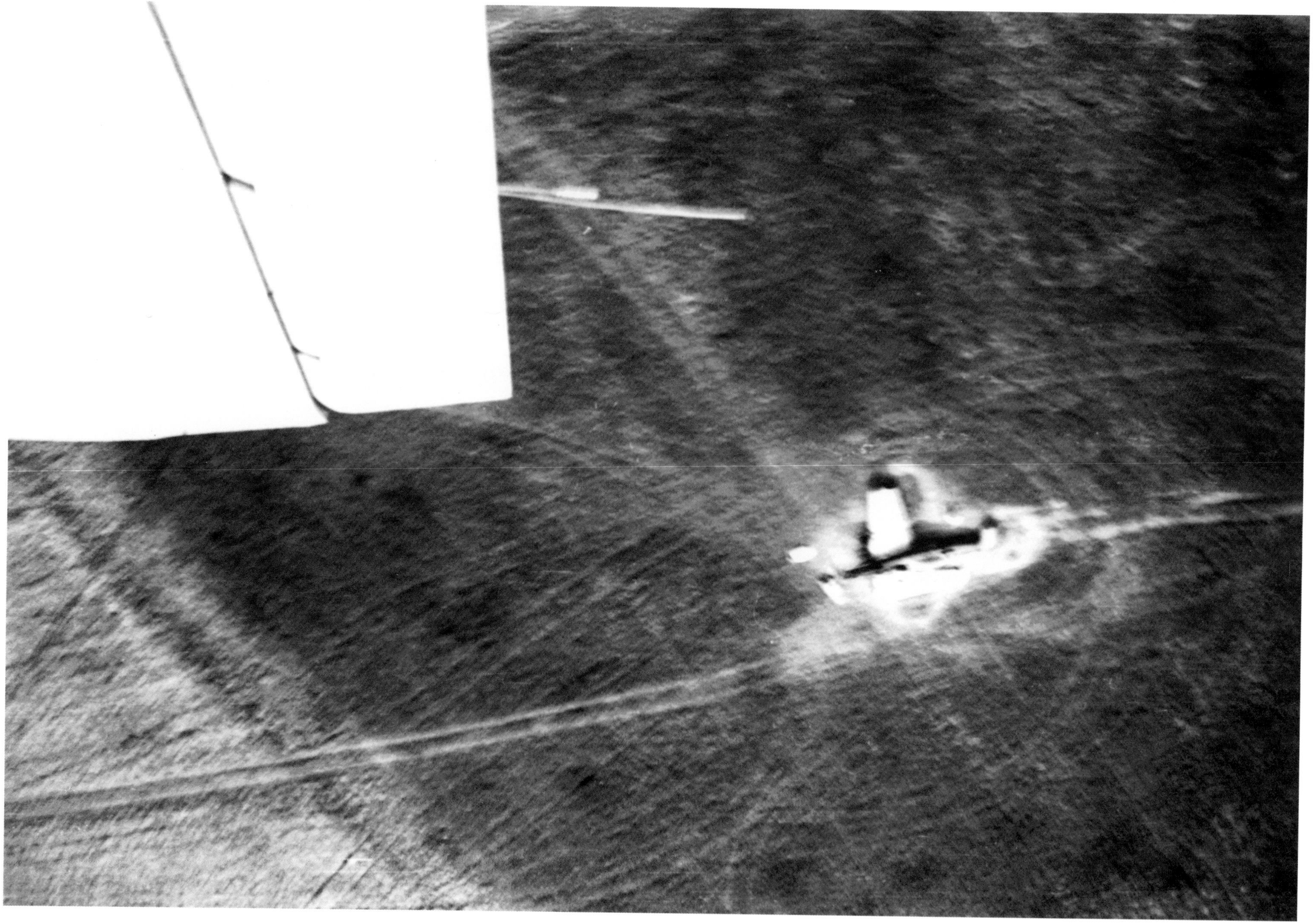

French Aircraft

This section shows abandoned allied aircraft in various states of damage, as well as relatively intact aircraft also. Of particular interest is the Caudron-Renault aircraft in a hangar with decidedly Stuka-like undercarriage. Which company 'lifted' the design from the other is not known. A somewhat unusual aircraft design nevertheless.

MS
406C1
N° 10 10

ÉFENSE DE FUMER
CAUDRON-
-RENAULT
ARER

Personnel

This section covers what might be termed the daily life of the *Staffel*. It shows in a comprehensive way all facets of a unit in action, from ground personnel going about their daily work to pilots 'relaxing' in deckchairs. Leisure time is also depicted, with officers testing/honing their skills on the firing range. *Staffelhunde* are in evidence, the silent witnesses to every flying unit's history, whose story will never be told. The diversity of photographs is such that to caption most would be to do them a disservice. They stand alone, and collectively, as mute testimony to a period in young men's lives that brought not only intense bonds of camaraderie, but also the stark reality of the brutality of war that was ultimately served upon them.

Werder

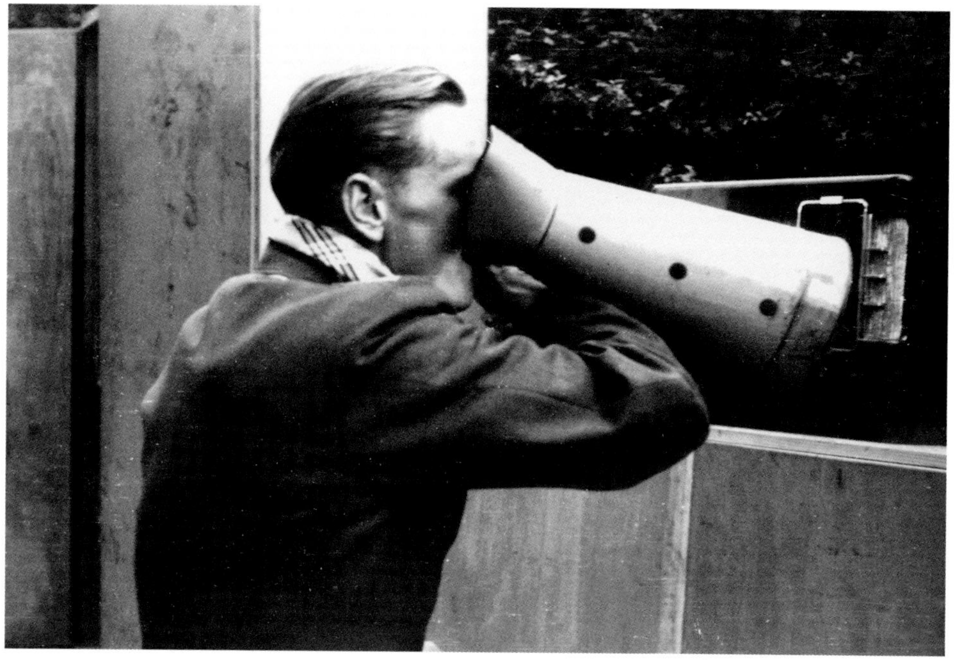

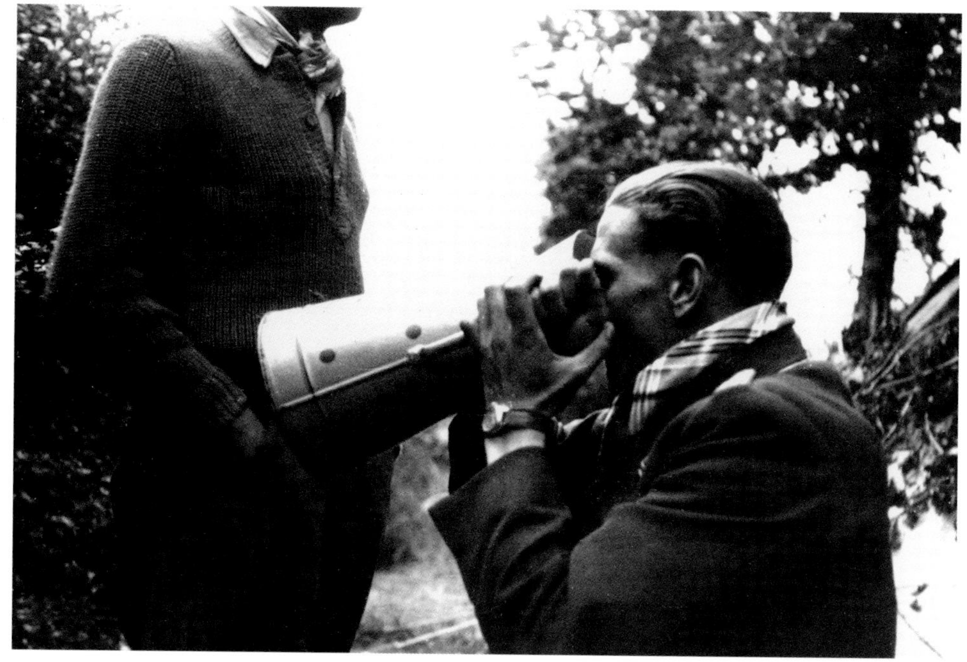

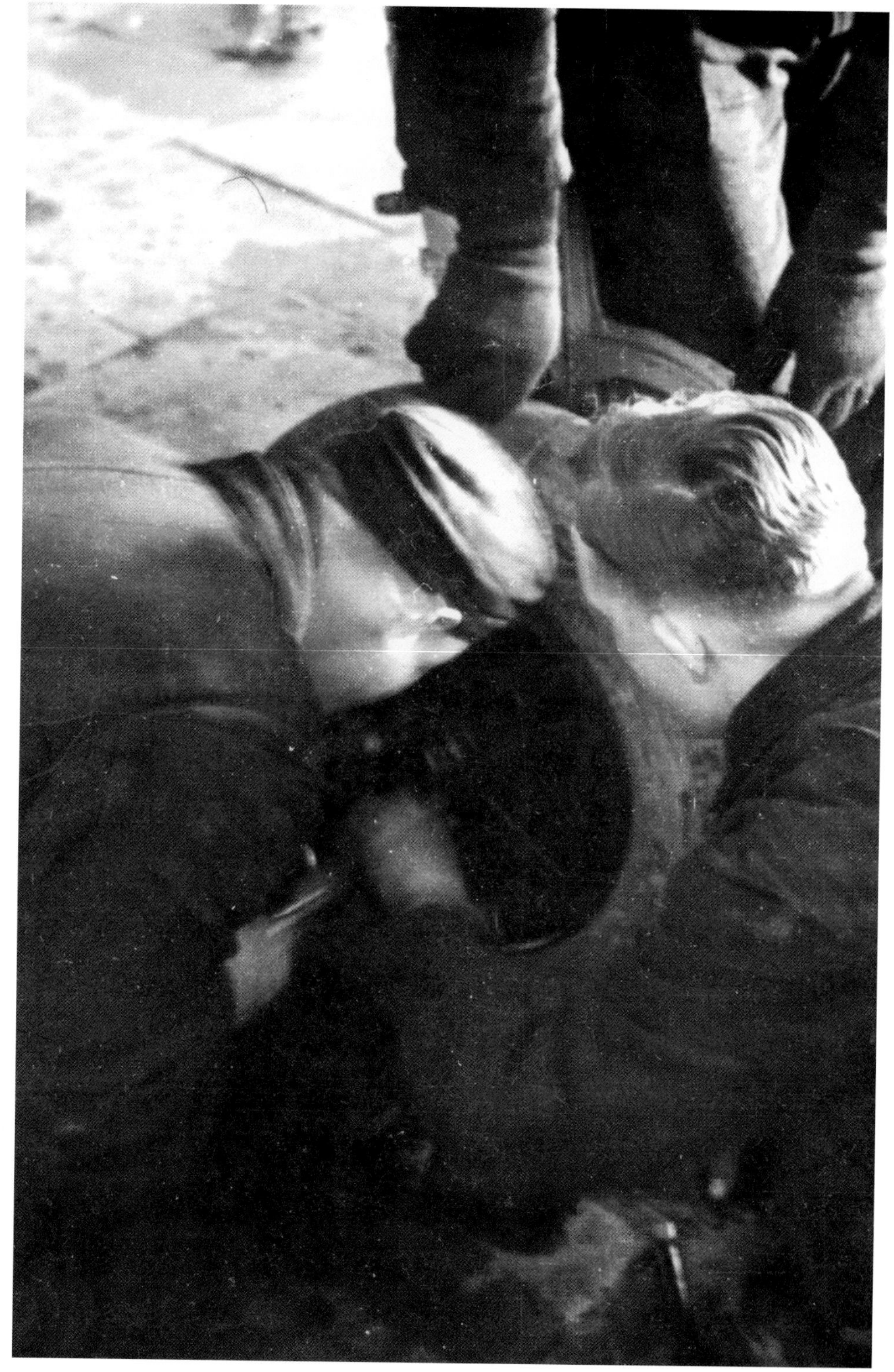

1528M1

902
S

Art zu rauchen

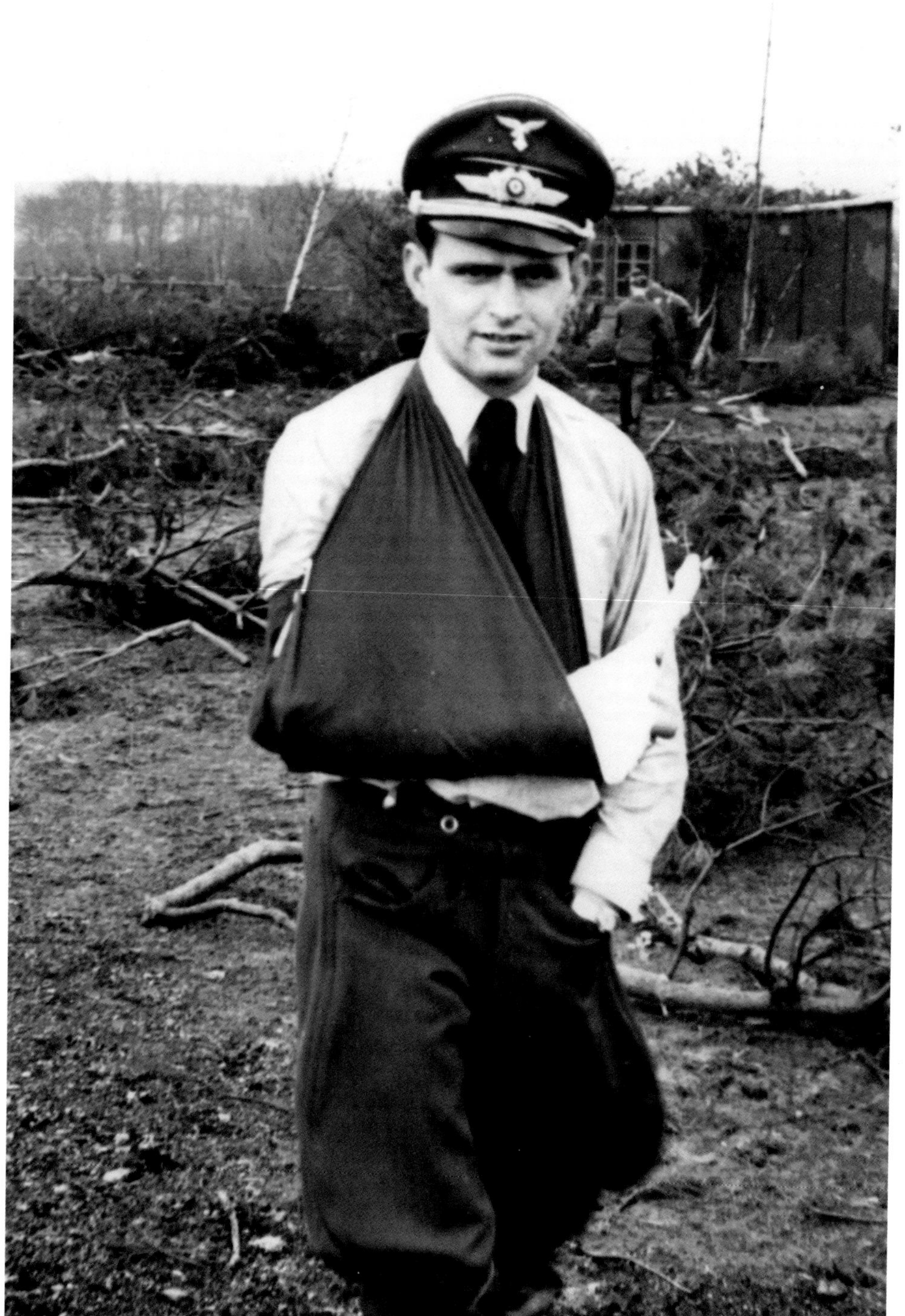

45

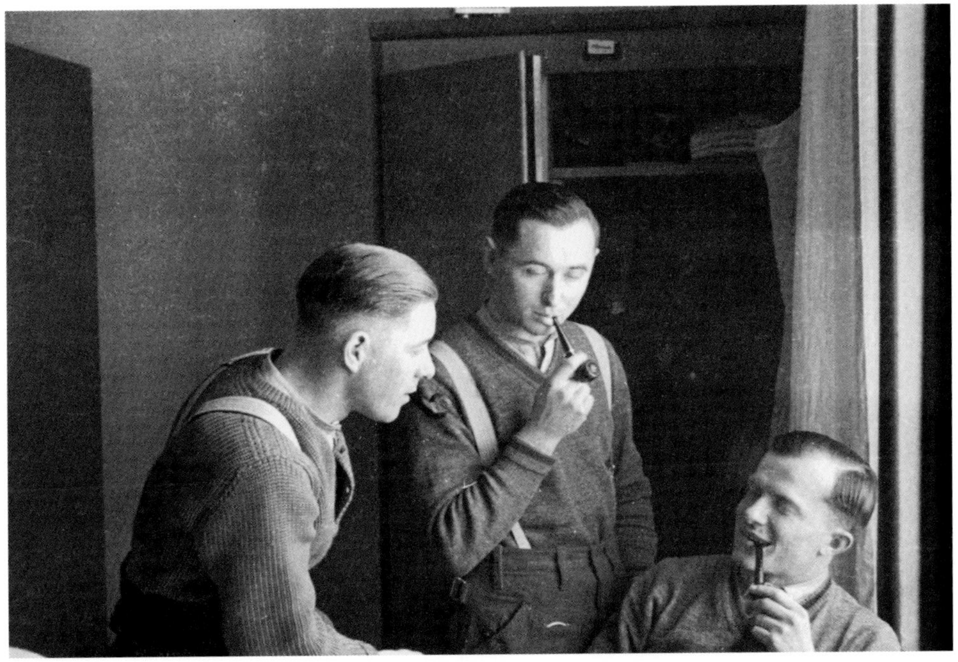

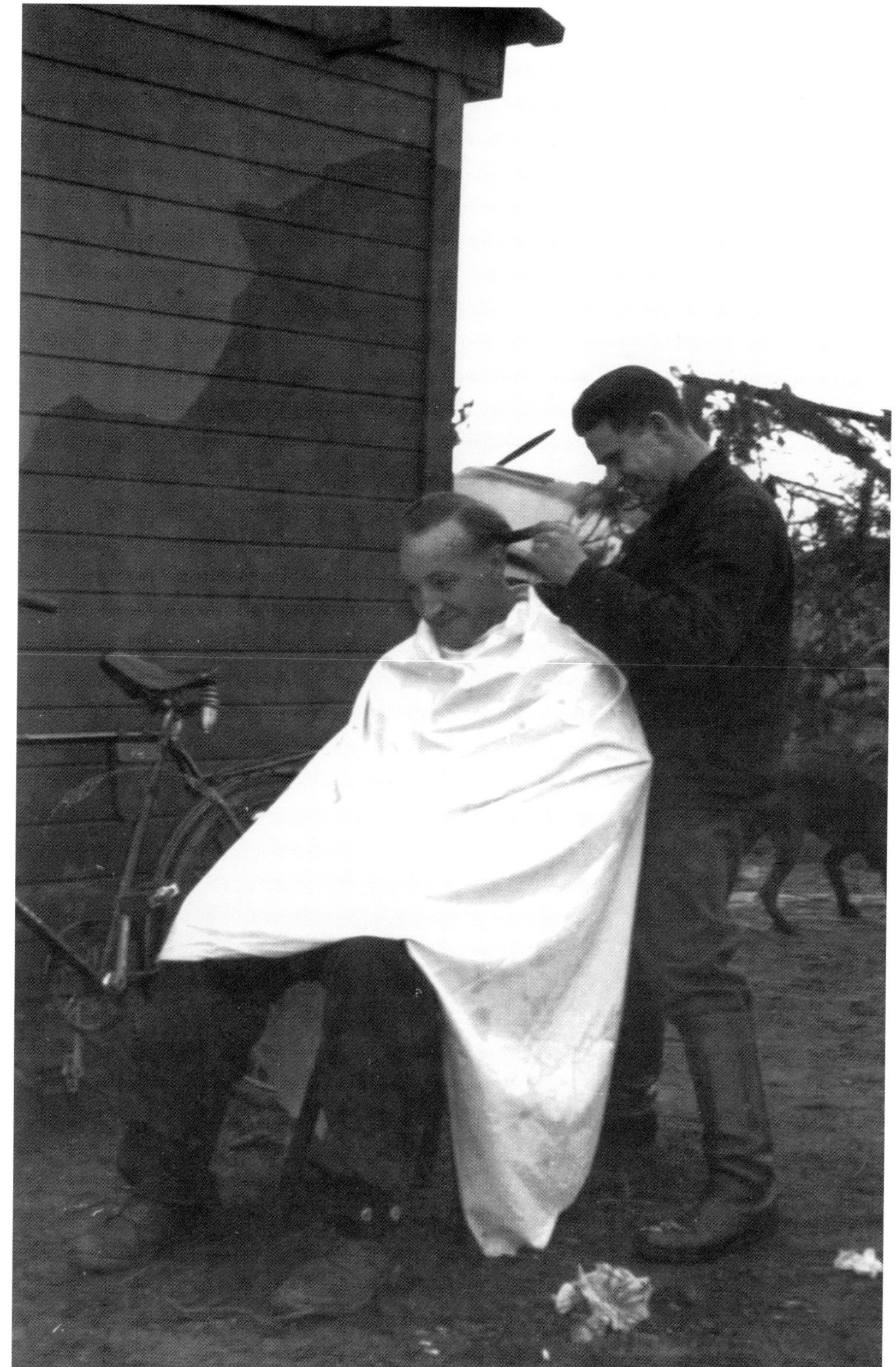

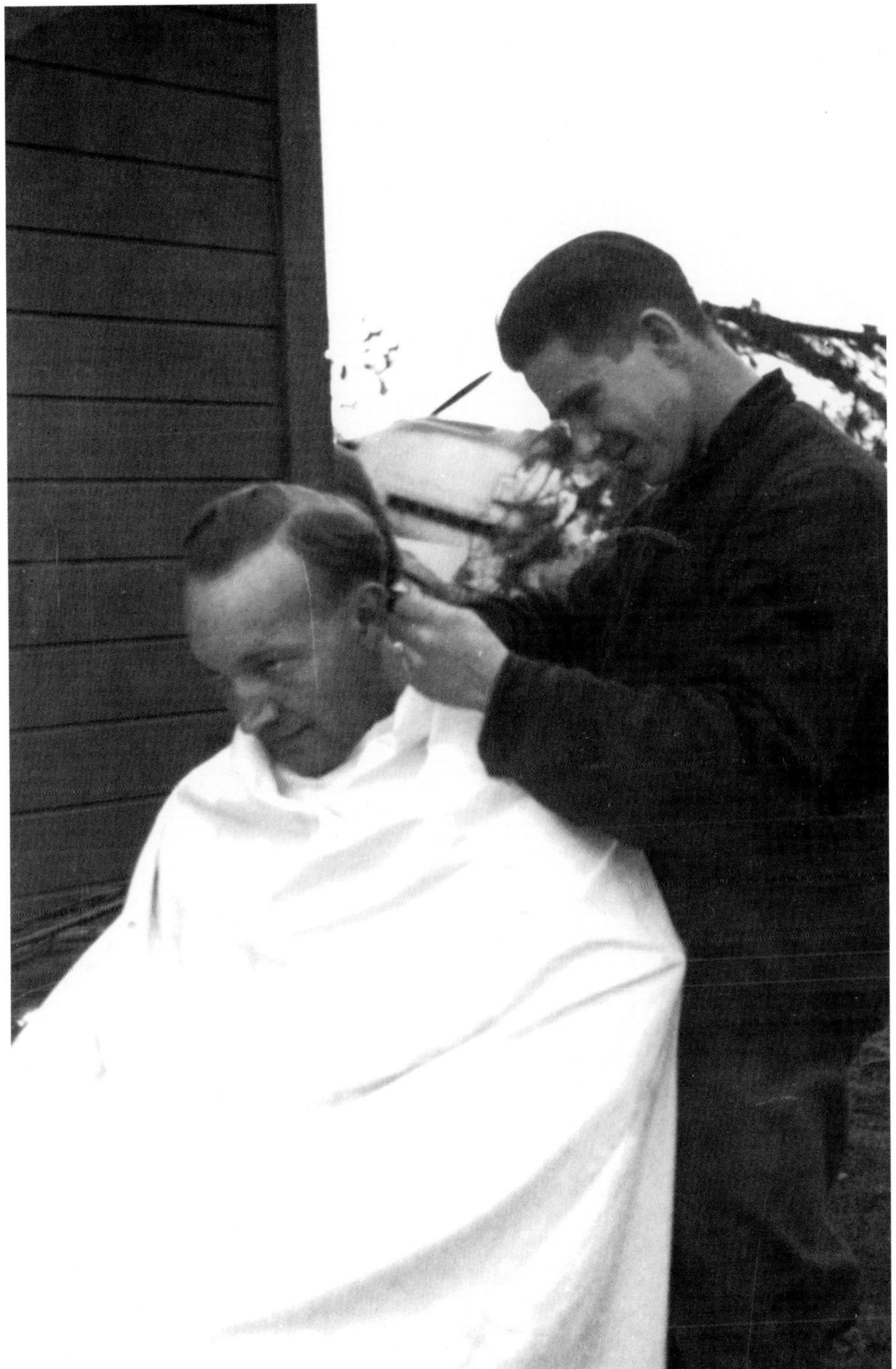

Population

This section shows scenes encountered by the *Staffel* as they progressed west during the spring campaign of 1940. Familiar views of lines of prisoners marching into captivity, and civilians fleeing along roads hoping to avoid falling under the control of advancing German forces.

HALTE!
CAFE
BIERES
WIELEMANS

AU PONT DU CANAL